# What Good Is a U?

amicus readers

1

by Marie Powell

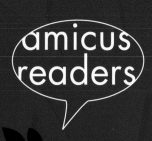

# Say Hello to Amicus Readers.

You'll find our helpful dog, Amicus, chasing a ball—to let you know the reading level of a book.

## 1

### Learn to Read

Frequent repetition, high frequency words, and close photo-text matches introduce familiar topics and provide ample support for brand new readers.

## 2

### Read Independently

Some repetition is mixed with varied sentence structures and a select amount of new vocabulary words are introduced with text and photo support.

## 3

### Read to Know More

Interesting facts and engagin art and photos give fluent readers fun books both for reading practice and to learn about new topics.

Amicus Readers are published by Amicus
P.O. Box 1329, Mankato, MN 56002
www.amicuspublishing.us

Library of Congress Cataloging-in-Publication Data

Powell, Marie, 1958-, author.
  What good is a U? / By Marie Powell.
    pages cm. -- (Vowels)
  Summary: "Beginning readers are introduced to the vowel U and its sounds and uses."-- Provided by publisher.
  ISBN 978-1-60753-712-0 (library binding)
  ISBN 978-1-60753-816-5 (ebook)
  1. Vowels--Juvenile literature. 2. English language--Vowels--Juvenile literature. I. Title.
  PE1157.P69446 2015
  428.1'3--dc23
                    2014045796

Photo Credits: Andreja Donko/Shutterstock Images, cover; Shutterstock Images, 1, 3, 13, 15, 16 (top left), 16 (bottom left); Cheryl Casey/Shutterstock Images, 4-5 Digital Vision/Photodisc/Thinkstock, 6; iStock/Thinkstock, 9; Danai Jetawattana/ iStock/Thinkstock, 10-11, 16 (bottom right); Aleksandar Grozdanovski/Shutterstoc Images, 16 (top right)

Produced for Amicus by The Peterson Publishing Company and Red Line Editorial.

Editor Jenna Gleisner
Designer Craig Hinton

Printed in Malaysia
10 9 8 7 6 5 4 3 2 1

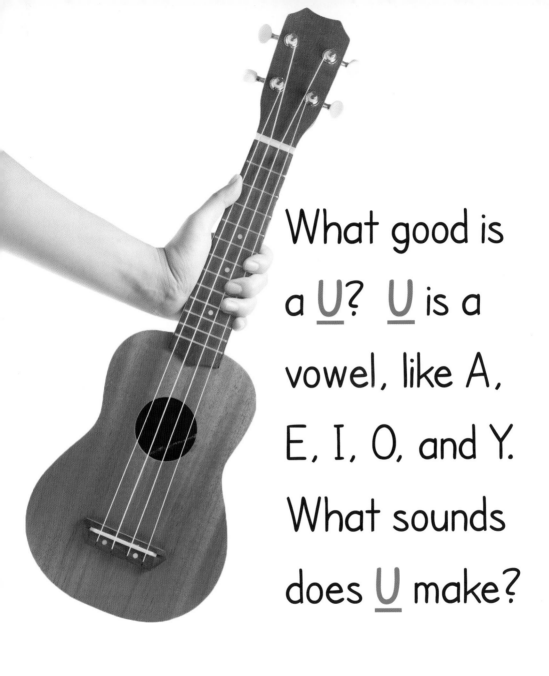

What good is a <u>U</u>? <u>U</u> is a vowel, like A, E, I, O, and Y. What sounds does <u>U</u> make?

U can have a long sound. Lucy plays a tune on her flute.

U can have a short sound.

Justin pounds a drum.

U can start a word.
Udo stands up. He plays
his ukulele.

U can come in the middle of a word. R<u>u</u>by and S<u>u</u>ki sing a d<u>ue</u>t.

U can make an oo sound.
It can come in the middle
or at the end of a word.
Lulu wears her tutu.

Our band is such fun! Will you join? U can be used to make many words.

# Vowel: U

Which words have a long <u>U</u> sound?

Which words have a short <u>U</u> sound?

## ukulele

## drum

## fun

## duet